Laurels

The Poetry of Long Island's Poets Laureate

Edited by James P. Wagner (Ishwa)

Laurels

Copyright © 2017 by Local Gems Press.

Edited by James P. Wagner (Ishwa)

Editorial Advisor: George Wallace

www.localgemspoetrypress.com

All rights reserved. No part of this book may be reproduced or transmitted in any form or by any means without written permission of the authors.

This book is dedicated to all those poets who serve as examples to other poets. The Laureates of our time...

Foreword

In the wake of the September 11 attacks great numbers of people longed for a place where they could find some solace. Not surprisingly, that place was poetry. Billy Collins, the former United States Poet Laureate, said, "[Poetry] provides a refuge from the din of public language." Furthermore he adds that public language speaks to the masses whereas poetry is "one person speaking to you."

When I introduced a resolution calling for the establishment of the position of Suffolk County Poet Laureate, I was met with some resistance by those legislators who deigned poetry to be of little importance. They underestimated the human need to make sense of the world and the human condition through art.

My legislative intent in creating the role of Poet Laureate in Suffolk County was to name a poet who would make poetry accessible to our residents by encouraging the publication of local writing and developing and attending forums where the public could enjoy live poetry readings. The task force formed by this legislation chose a published poet who actively participated in a supportive community of poets and who was committed to expanding the public's appreciation and enjoyment of poetry.

The first Poet Laureate of Suffolk County, George Wallace, exceeded our expectations. He attended events throughout the county and beyond, he spoke at libraries and schools and advised the County regarding activities that educate and entertain the public through poetry.

The poets laureate that have succeeded George continue to contribute their talents and energy to our county residents and I am proud that I played a small part in effecting this great outcome. Even better that shortly after the founding of the Suffolk County Poet Laureate, our neighbor Nassau County followed suit, providing Nassau with the same poetic enrichment.

The poems contained in these pages are beautiful, eloquent and relevant. I congratulate all of you for sharing your talents and time with us through your active participation in our communities and for your extraordinary poetry.

My best to you all,

~ Vivian Viloria Fisher

Suffolk County Legislator 1999 - 2011
Deputy Presiding Officer 2006 -2011

Table of Contents

Suffolk County Poets Laureate 1

George Wallace 2
   A Simple Blues With A Few Intangibles 4
   Jonesing With Moses On The High Tide Line 5
   Like A Peach Tree Blossoming In Winter Rain 6
   You Have Spoken To Me 7
   Late Night Ballad For Runaway Lovers 8
   Heaven Is A Rubber-Toed Butterfly 10
   Offroad Fourwheel Busted Up Collarbone Rollbar
      Miss America 11

Dr. David B. Axelrod 14
   Caution: Cancer Causes Poetry 16
   Curing Rilke 17
   Celebrate Good Times 18
   Peg Leg Bates 20
   The Dirty Old Man 22
   Sun Worship 24
   Surprises 25

Tammy Nuzzo-Morgan 26
   Prose In Abstract 28
   In 29
   Bone 31
   This Is Not Your Poem 32
   Maybe Someday I Will Get It Right 33
   Breath An Irish Sky 35
   The Blues Has 365 Hands 36
Ed Stever 37
   Liftoff 39
   Missives From Africa 41
   The Wedge & Winds of War 43
   A Story of Fish & Blood 45
   Drinking With Disney Characters 46
   The Tower 47
   Family Vacations 48
Pramila Venkateswaran 50
   Walls 52
   Chipped Crockery 55
   Flight 56
   Lisp 57
   Black and White Pictures of Death Camps 58
   Mother Teresa's Sari 59
   Sweatshop 60

Robert Savino 61
   Trail of Seeds 63
   Occupational Therapy 65
   Breakfast With Sophia 66
   Composite Color 67
   It's Not Always Black and White 69
   Make No Revision 71

Nassau County Poets Laureate 73
Maxwell Corydon Wheat Jr. 74
   Snow Buntings 76
   Orb Weaver 77
   Acid Rain 78
   The Lamps of America Were Illuminated With Whale Oil 79
   Veteran 81
   Harbor Seals In Winter 82
   Lycopodium 83
Gayl Teller 84
   Jasmine 85
   Memorial Day 86
   Three Weavers 89
   Worn-Out Walking Shoes 90

Moving Day 92
Linda Opyr 94
   Pavarotti Is Dead 96
   Turtles 97
   Why Me 98
   The Gulls 99
   The Stranger 100
   Fogbound 101
   Grey Clouds 102
Mario Susko 103
   Life 105
   Checkpoint 107
   Plots of Life, Plots of Death 109
   A Shortcut 111
   Conversion 113
   Homeward Bound 115
Lorraine Conlin 117
   As Good As Bread 119
   Brass Ring 121
   Grapevine 123
   Looking For Nina 125
   Marlboro Man 127
   Hands 129
   Rockaway Of My Heart 131

Suffolk County Poets Laureate

George Wallace

Suffolk County Poet Laureate 2003-2005

What is a laureate? It's been over a quarter of a century since I returned to Long Island -- the place of my birth and childhood -- and busied myself trying to answer that question. 25+ years working as a 'citizen poet' in the midst of an incomparable assemblage of writers, working hard to grow our mutual association into a true community with shared purpose and common cause.

Of course in my two decades away from home I'd accumulated plenty of the perspective and experience necessary to do my part. Training and practice as a community organizer, a couple of years in the Peace Corps and a succession of volunteer opportunities on three continents gave me a foundation for action.

Building on that foundation has been easy, thanks to the countless writers or the region who have worked with me unselfishly toward that goal all these years -- and continue to do so. The laureates who share these pages with me in this anthology are among those. As are the laureates yet to be named, not yet recognized with the title but deserving of it just the same.

Here's to many more years working with my fellow poets on Long Island, laureates all, making sure our mutual association is a productive and meaningful one.

It's been a great ride over the last quarter century. I'm ready to sign up for another 25.

A Simple Blues With A Few Intangibles

simple blues with a few intangibles
what johnny had been playing all
night long, all night long & all his
life in a one room walk up beating
on a steam pipe with the heel of
his shoe, nothing much on his mind
except work the back room, a beat
sort of gentleman with a chill in the
bebop, a blues sort of gentleman,
positively anarchistic & wise o man
what a cool bohemian & beat to the
bone -- how he worked that tune, no
more no less than the music of the
universe passing thru the man, from
the gods & for them & for the people
too, it was always about the people,
johnny crooned, running new chords
& old chords & no chords over his
tongue like the midas of midnight,
in the solitude of his own sweet
madness, at home with the moon

Jonesing With Moses On The High Tide Line

me my girl & the road --one foot on the dash
the other in paradise

ace high flying carpet top down trunk latch
yes this wreck's a rust bucket

battleship but me & my girl in the front are
flying boy flying on the high

beam jonesing with moses on the high tide
line got our eyes on the oceanic

prize we are stoking the dream machine we
are american we are made we got

audio dynamite & the sun's rising over the
atlantic got all the time in the

world darling let's bow out let's cut loose let's
throw it over get it done one way

all the way this stone age jive'll never get old
& it will never die

Like A Peach Tree Blossoming In Winter Rain

i have never regretted the noise a city makes when it becomes too big to hold itself in, when the lights turn green and streets come alive, i mean -- when the music trapped inside a city gets to be too much, like bottled wine, and has to come out

or the small noises a city makes, singing to itself at dawn, when no one much is listening, i have never regretted that, the forgiveness song a city sings to itself, more beautiful than the yank of fiddle, than the blown pride of flute or jackhammer

the small sounds of a city no one can hear, amid all the noises, when i am listening i mean, your voice 'singing in all the world,' like paul eluard said, like birds singing in an awning at dawn -- no, i have never regretted that

it is a new year, i could blossom out from these walls that bind me yet, from this jazz that holds me in -- it is a new year, i am not done yet, i could sing a song, for anyone who's sober enough to listen

like a peach tree blossoms out in winter rain
i could blossom out yet, with your song

You Have Spoken To Me

yes, you have spoken to me, as in a dream
i mean, like a flock of starlings speaks to the
wind, as the wind speaks the inevitability of
oceans to trees, as a grove of trees gives it
all back to the wind, patternweaver, dream-
speaker, poem of the endless air, endlessly
green, your voice also, sea hillock and wave,
bleating, mad as thistle, yet comforting and
green and green, your sweet dampness, the
mysterious vowels of your flight, coordinated
beyond measure, poured like black wine, your
metaphor of going and going and coming back,
dancing dark as a winter cloud of starlings --
over grass and tree, over the green sea of me

Late Night Ballad For Runaway Lovers

Play it like it's love
Play it like it's brand new
Play it like it's you and
Me, Blanche et noire
A mystery in the
Gershwin, honey it is
Three a.m. & there's
Groceries everywhere
No one here to tell us stay
So weary so weary
But it ain't time
& no quit in us,
Give me your hand
Play it like it's 1943
There's a war on
Quinine water
& Tanqueray
Play it like his world's
a Crown of kisses,
Why is it so hard
For you to smile
Night is a napkin
In solitude's hand,
Folding in on itself,

Indiana is a harvest moon
And this ain't Gary
This ain't Kokomo
This is a can of corn
At a corner bar on
West 118th & the city
Never glowed so bright

Heaven Is A Rubber-Toed Butterfly

the man who scales a mountain in search of
paradise will end up in the mayonnaise jar
the prize is inside the box baby just ask the
crackerjack man he knows and will further
more tell you ad nauseum anydamn thing
you're looking for, right here in your little
old heart o it's a free country all right take
what you need and god bless the taker, man
is not made of bread alone search the kif hike
the high himalayas seek out the lost land of mu
deep dive into frigging atlantis if you want
to there are no falafels in paradise no pot of
gold in the footlocker eternity is flat as a wrist
watch at dawn but it keeps on ticking so don't
cop that attitude with me -- boom baby boom
and tick tock baby – one minute everything's
a-ok, next thing you know you're at the end of
the rainbow roller coaster face to face with
mister death -- so lean to the left lean to the
right have a good time falafels have wings
pancakes are round-- heaven is a rubber
toed butterfly and god is a jack in the box
he'll spring right up and bite your nose

Offroad Fourwheel Busted Up Collarbone Rollbar Miss America

she loved to dunebuggy she loved to ride she loved to be outside herself to spit and to cry to hop like a toad to burn like a barn – o shoot like novocaine -- she spit in the bushes she spit on the mountaintop on the prairie on the bayou into the mouthhole of the universal universe –

she loved shenandoah mississippi oklahoma sioux -- she loved hotwheel all weather souterrain space jam

rain rain rain -- top down hood up piston busting woman of the blue sky her tietack shoe shine shotgun shack home on the range, and o! she loved her own thick hair like nobody's business she combed it back she let it go wild she tossed it back

like a steel drum band like a back door catholic prophylactic mormon figure eight little miss pagan America crazy drunk entitled mademoiselle

crazy drunk or spying on her own sweet self -- o no o no, o nono NO miss fourth of july campfire rollbar america! the embers don't go out on you, no not on YOU, nor the lights on broadway nor the poolhall lights or the jailhouse lights no not the junk yard lights or the headlights or the supernatural supermarket lights all night long in the parking lot –

& o her mulish temper & o her talking back and her racked up men with metallic skin – skinny men, fat men, muscle headed men, sheets of gold -- no one could stop her no titanium grease gun jake no feedbag joe no coke dust dipstick tin shield sawdust sheriff

and here's what's important -- she loved herself, her body her muscle her calves her skin her ankle-thigh hip high heel boots she shuttered and waved like the prairie grass she secretly wanted to be – she loved to be outside herself, she loved and she loved and she needed to be loved –

she shoved it around she shook it out -- got took got lost, got rediscovered wasted and found -- ripped open given away put up on a pedestal took for a ride stolen in the night

she yanked it all out, every ounce of it, the flesh the earth the river the rain the red rock forest of oak, she plummeted like eagles she grew like silver corn she spooned up asphalt and plowed it back under and trucked it away and bombed and bombed and bombed, unfairly unwisely arrogantly (which is normal and faulty and human too) and acted foolish when she wanted to and wise when you didn't expect it off-road fourwheel busted up collarbone rollbar miss america tossed her helmet fifty feet in the air and caught it in her right hand just like that! big yahoo! pop fly sixpack beanbag woman, headphones blaring, dung busting batshit crazy headed off to anywhere doomed as a devildog little miss american paradise! leaped out of the dark & into the sun

Dr. David B. Axelrod

Suffolk County Poet Laureate 2007-2009

    I arrived on Long Island an academic wanderer with New England roots. Now, I'm a Florida poet with a Long Island heart. When I moved to Long Island in 1969, fresh from the Iowa Writers Workshops with my M.F.A., I thought I was just passing through. I was hired to put creative writing into the curriculum at Suffolk College, but I was also a Ph.D. student at SUNY Stony Brook, so I thought I'd go on to another, bigger school thereafter.

But Long Island turned into very fertile ground—close to NYC but rural, even agricultural as I went east; infused with the ocean and the Sound. As good or better, Long Island was teaming with poets and writers. Within a few months I became friends with Louis Simpson, David and Rose Ignatow, Aaron Kramer, Diana Chang. In 1976, I and a group of friends started Writers Unlimited Agency, Inc. (WU), a not-for-profit writers co-op and, I became the sponsor of hundreds of literary events. I lived in Walt's back yard—and for all the years on Long Island, I had the Hamptons as my hangout. Suffice it to say, I loved my poetic home and prospered there.

All of this is to say, I was honored and grateful to accept the title of Suffolk County Poet Laureate (2007-2009).

Now that I've moved away, I've made new friends and am grateful for their acceptance. I'm Volusia County Poet Laureate (2015-2019) and director of a new non-profit, Creative Happiness Institute, Inc. What I miss most about Suffolk is not its proximity to NYC. I don't miss the ocean because Daytona Beach, Florida, has its own exquisite shore. But I do miss the diversity and vitality of Long Island's writers. I know good writers here in Florida and meet some fine visitors to the area, but poetry is a core value on Long Island.

Caution: Cancer Causes Poetry

So many people—academics,
probation officers, cab drivers,
waitresses—all writing poetry,
lamenting lost breasts; glad
to be rid of festering colons
despite the colostomy bags.
Holding notebooks, iPads,
waiting for open mics,
proclaiming remission.
Or, confessing metastases,
Consoling themselves they
fought it the best way they could.
But wait, now you think I am
unsympathetic. You are mistaken.
I am the one who advocates
the healing power of poetry,
encourages first chapbooks,
believes even beginners should
be taken seriously. But, for all
the lines written on order forms,
hotel notepads, tiny qwerty
keyboards, I'm tired of how
cancer causes poetry when
we need much more than
empathy. We need a cure.

Curing Rilke

*("If my devils leave me, I'm afraid
my angels will take flight as well.")*
So said Rainer Maria Rilke,
but he was haunted by disembodied
hands and I often dwell in fantasy.
Was it Byron who said he saw
the ghosts of impending imbecility?
Now, we live long enough to fear
forgetting "me." And there's no cure
beyond stupefying pills forced on
the senile and elderly. For trauma,
perhaps there's therapy: a short
interview, a trusting induction,
and poof—release, but leaving what?
An infant's early yearnings? A scholar's
tabula rasa? I shall dwell in these
dark, familiar thoughts until there is
nothing left of me. If my devils
leave me, will my angels also flee?

Celebrate Good Times

Why my mother didn't like
celebrations is complicated.
No holiday was sacred. Beyond
an ethnic antipathy to Christmas,
she joked that Jewish Valentines
Day was February 15, when
the candy was half priced, laughing
equally at cheap-Jew stereotypes
and "all that sentimental tripe."
For her wedding, she and my dad
eloped—a simple justice of the peace—
forever infuriating her Orthodox
in-laws. Even for her fiftieth anniversary,
barely a mention—though her marriage
was sound. For ninety-one years, her
birthdays weren't important. Was it
child-of-the-Depression frugality?
She squeezed a nickel until
the buffalo choked—but, actually,
was very generous. Perhaps,
she thought herself unworthy.
Though she painted portraits better
than some famous artists, she never
advertised her talents. Self effacing?

A little, but most of all she told me
that, deep in her atheist heart,
she knew, "Life is no big deal.
Live it and be done." Who are we
to celebrate, as if we are a gift
in some God's creation?

Peg Leg Bates

Peg Leg Bates lost his leg
to a cotton gin when he was
twelve. I lost all trust from
infancy—wondering wordlessly
when I would die. Peg Leg
loved to tap dance and got
famous for leaping five feet
in the air to land on his wooden
leg. I got beaten first then
sexually abused landing
somewhere in nightmares
later because you don't
forget that stuff. Bates
appeared on Ed Sullivan's
show twenty-one times, even
danced for the King of England.
All I want to do is entertain
myself with you. Mine is
a dance of a different kind.
Sure, I have a visible handicap.
You could call Peg Leg
a freak show but that would
be unkind. When he danced
it was graceful, remarkable.

You didn't feel his pain.
You didn't think of how they
cut off his mangled leg on his
mother's kitchen table.
Just let me dance—with you.
The abusers have left the room

The Dirty Old Man

Left alone by the death
of a spouse, a dirty old
man needs love. Long
in the fang but short on
stamina, stirred by an
ancient lust, he watches
young women passing by.
An old man, bald, bearded,
who has bought a fast car,
dressed in his Bill Blass
blazer, ventures into
a bar, his pocket filled
with cash. There are women
less than half his age who
let him buy them drinks.
One tells him tales of abuse.
"Daddy beat me and so did
my ex." An old man takes her
home, lets her use the bathroom,
waits in his boxer shorts on
the edge of the bed. Next
morning, after he's scrambled
her eggs topped with Velveeta,
she promises they can meet

at the same bar, soon, but
doesn't set a time. There
are polite goodbyes and her
exit. Reaching for the Old Spice,
an old man notices missing
bottles of his dead wife's last
painkillers kept in the medicine
cabinet in case his own life
isn't worth living anymore.

Sun Worship

The dermatologist burns a dozen spots
off me with liquid nitrogen. For all I
know, at sixty bucks a pop, he could just be
making this up to pay for his Mercedes.
He tells me the sun is dangerous—wear
a hat, use tons of sunscreen. I'm stupid.
I still love the sun, luxuriating in my
backyard with a book and iced tea.
They tell me it's a hole in the ozone
or maybe a solar eruption that sends
radiation straight at me. Basal cell
this and squamous that and oh, the dreaded
melanoma. Perspiration streams down
my solar plexus. I'm oiled and browned.
No one can tell me Vitamin D stands for death.

Surprises

(with thanks to Dr. Marvin Levine)
For some, there are no surprises.
Their Goddess watches over them
while others prefer a bearded old
man and think everything is
destined. If the Reaper opens my door
and gestures toward me, I'll laugh.
"What are you laughing at, you
damned fool?" Death will say,
"I'm here for your soul."
"Given a lifetime of doubt, if
you are real, think of all the other
possibilities," says me.
"You aren't listening," he or
she might say, "It's the big one
and hey, maybe even hell."
But I've been married twice
before—which may explain my
lack of faith—and both ex-
wives told me to go to hell.
For me, life is full of surprises.

Tammy Nuzzo-Morgan

Suffolk County Poet Laureate 2009-2011

I am currently enrolled in the Doctorial Interdisciplinary Program at Union Institute & University, in the Humanities & Culture concentration. My dissertation topic is: The Healing Power of Poetry: The Creative Process. The workshop portion of my dissertation will encourage the artistic expression of personal traumatic and emotional voyage to be the conduit to create poetry in a positive and proactive manner. I believe we all carry ghosts; admittedly or not.

Serving the poetry community was an honor. For two years listening, communicating and learning were the gifts given to me when I was appointed by my predecessors. The grassroots poetry movement is where my words flow from, and find academia stymies my creative outlet.

Prose In Abstract

Be my cowbell shaking blue, green raining love wet.
Be my coffee mug filled with shining smell.
Take hold the buzzing words dripping from my ear.
Finger touch my explaining smile, mow yesterday into today.

Stay with me my tree fort love.
Wash piglets of sadness clean, making room for oranging leaves and burning dirt.
Wrap us in spider webs of dew; let the sun bear witness to our joining.

Hold out your river hand allowing silver fish entry.
I will sway daylong singing the Hail Mary of love songs with my seaweed lungs.

In

for Robert Long

So this is supposed to be the great metaphor for the gotta-get-to-fers that want the pain to stop like a shot of morphine. Like a visit from Morphosis, who brings dreams that become realty even for a temporary time. A place where a red & golden dragonfly morphs into that perfect person with all the answers to all your questions, & suspended reality becomes that higher plane of existence & only the most holy dwell.

But still you stand there, with your nose pressed against the window- pane, unable to explain why. Why you cannot find your way in, into the maze through the haze of the days that have blinded your vision from seeing the path that the children trot down, as they play hop-scotch.

All you do is stuff your hands into your pockets that are full of stuff that you protect as if it were delicacies that you were able to take to the table & serve up as part of a meal for the soul, but you know deep down that all it is is another slice of you that you gave up to be part of that scene that dances at the club to beat that drives the grind and produces the sweat on the necks and backs and arms of the women and men who are searching, searching, searching.

And you walk away spent, another day carved away from your Thanksgiving Day turkey of dreams because you did not stand up for them; those with no tongues or arms or legs to those who wield the power without grace.

So now you go home & lie down & watch T V & hope to blur out the images that define your mind, or pick up a book that holds this poem & take a look and play hide and seek within the lines & finally think you know what it all means, but it is not here, but within you.

You are the poet, the Morphosis, the god of dreams. Spin that red and golden dragonfly into that perfect person. Turn her into a flaming redhead with flowing hair; drape her in a dress of spun gold. Give her wings to fly you out and over the city. Look upon all that stirs below. Swoop down into the alleyways and door-ways and subways and witness the pulse of the people. Remember and write.

Bone

[my dog buried his b[one] so deep that he n[or] I could f[in]d it]we [s[hopp[ed]] for a new [on]e! He [l]ike]d] it very [[m][u][c][h]] and [I] could [[no]w] [sle]ep] [[so]und]ly f[or] t[he] [f[i]rst] ti[me] in [a] [[wee]k] [an]d he d[ream]t of bones [[[and]]] [to]ys and [l[on]g] w[a]lks on the [be][a]ch]

This Is Not Your Poem

It doesn't have a damn thing to do with you.
So do not be concerned with what is written in it.

It isn't about you at all,
doesn't hold a fragment of you in it.

This is not your poem.
It never was or will be.

It doesn't care one thing about you.
As a matter of fact I think I heard it chuckle
that you thought it was your poem.

It contains not one molecule of you or what you are about.
It is totally unrelated to you and the world you live in.

I overheard the other poems whispering about how
this is not your poem.

Maybe Someday I Will Get It Right

I forgot to close the window near the book case and bring in the cat and roll up the windows in the faded green clunker I call my car in the oil stained drive, and get the flashlight new batteries, just in case of another week-long blackout, and fill a few gallons of water and let out the dog before it came down in sheets. I forgot to tell you I need you.

I forgot to cut back the Montauk Daises and cover the pool and store away the grill and pack away the lounge cushions, the ones with white and blue stripes the ones you hate and the ones I love, and crank down the squeaky brown picnic table umbrella; the one the yellow jackets seem drawn to and put Michael's school project Adirondack chair into the shed before the leaves were done falling and walking became a trick we both watched to see if the other could do. I forgot to tell you I want you.

I forgot to salt the drive and put the shovels near the front door, and get the winter clothes: mittens, gloves, hats and scarves; including the ones I crocheted with brown and orange yarn, and the sweat shirts; the ones we got from the Giants game in 1998, before the blizzard hit our home like a tidal wave.

I forgot tell you I love you.

I forgot. I forgot. I forgot.

I forgot to fill the bird feeder and plant the red tulip bulbs, and lime the lawn and put a fresh coat of paint on the mailbox and hose off the screens leaning them against the wooden shingles of our single story home, just as my mother had and her mother had before her, and put the house plants out for air before the Robins arrived to pull worms up from their slumber.

I forgot to tell you how I hurt. I forgot to tell you I dream. I forgot to tell you I was wrong. I forgot to leave the porch light on, just in case you return.

Breath An Irish Sky

Where Willows don't weep
and trout dance with the fly fisher
in the ripples of the Liffey,
I watch the cosmos.
New bridges are built in my heart and
Wicklow heather is in bloom. Neither king,
nor queen walk the halls of Carbury
castle, which shelters sheep, ghosts, me.

I walk miles to be in the long room, where
joy falls like rain, where I am replenished.
Where foggy dew blankets the hills and
flocks settle down with the moon.

I will rest in the ferns at Glendalough,
where echoes of monks' prayers can still
be heard, where foxglove-speckled forest
remembers and the water fall whispers.

Tupelo Honey keeps playing in my mind,
while Portumna calls to me. I think I will go.
Where moss clings to smoke stacks, and
the Kingfisher dips wing into the Shannon.

The Blues Has 365 Hands

for Michael

The blues has 365 hands and
points gnarled fingers straight at me,
wags that I walk instead of run,
drums out the days I waste.

The blues has 365 hands and
clenches, taking aim at my belly,
pounds the table, demanding me to answer,
waves me off when I do.

The blues has 365 hands and
slaps me out of my coma,
flips their tall boys up in contempt,
signs, "How dare you?"

The blues has 365 hands and
claws nails along my face,
taps the keys of my phone, searching,
are stained with the wash of regret.

The blues has 365 hands and
counts out the 6,572 days you have been gone,
strokes my bowed head,
folds themselves in prayer.

Ed Stever

Suffolk County Poet Laureate 2011-2013

Being the Suffolk County Poet Laureate, 2011-13 was an honor that I had never expected, nor anticipated, even though I had been writing since 1986. During that time, I also started a group, The Poetry Theater Ensemble, with friends I often acted with, integrating music into the piece. That inching toward becoming the laureate was grand fun, though I never foresaw such a possibility of inhabiting that position. I was just enjoying myself, and that was good enough for me. When I was finally asked by the prior laureate, Tammy Nuzzo-Morgan, if I were interested in the post, I was surprised, but certainly elated! She claims at first I said no, though I don't remember, but I'm sure she is correct. Shortly thereafter, I retired from full-time employment and that was what enabled me to feel I could then properly dedicate myself to the position. Of course, former laureates all had a say in who would be elected, and I am extremely grateful to those who supported me. And I must say that initially I thought two years was a lifetime; nonetheless, it seemed to roar by.

During that time, I made numerous friends and met wonderful people on the journey, to whom, and for which, I shall always be grateful. I was glad to have been able to contribute to so many different lives -- helping out at the Northport VFW, aiding a fellow poet who lost her home to fire, and numerous other occasions that enriched every moment of my term. I thank everyone who made it a reality, especially those who helped younger poets, just as I did.

So, the next time you see this old ex-laureate on the poetry scene, say hi. I'll give it right back to ya. Pax vobiscum.

Liftoff

I try to fold my ancient mother into the front seat of the car
without piercing her parchment flesh on the sharp edges of the door
or bashing her head against the roof. I hold her head like the police do,
helping the convicted into the car.

I buckle her in but she forgets to remove her hands and she is strapped down,
arms and pocketbook trapped, so I tap the release, and we start all over again.

As we drive, she asks, "So are you in any plays now?"
I tell her about my roles in Romeo and Juliet and she says,
"Oh that sounds like fun."

Ten seconds later she asks, "So are you in any plays now?"
and we start all over again.

We arrive at my sister's house to see my brother,
in from California for obvious reasons.

I open my mother's door and pull feet and legs out,

hoping her upper body pivots too, without her cracking in half.

I try to place her feet on the driveway for proper balance, but she says, "No that's not right," and we start all over again.

I clutch her beneath broken pinions and say, "One, two, three!" and lift.
But life resists.

She collapses back into the seat and we start all over again.

We succeed on our second attempt and WE HAVE LIFTOFF!
And as I shuttle her to the house under the cold black blanket of the night,
the ancient stars in their youth mock us with their brilliance.

I hope the Buddhists and the Hindus are right about reincarnation,
and that we can start all over again, this time my mother as a sleek and bounding gazelle.

Missives From Africa

In emails from Kenya,
my daughter, Kim, tries
to quell my anxieties,
by writing, "We sleep out
on the veranda at night.
But *don't worry*, I check my shoes
for scorpions in the morning,"
and "No, we swim on *our* side
of the river. The crocodiles
sunbathe on the *opposite* bank,"
and "Yes, the camel spiders
are as big as your hand,"
and "Yes, they are arachnids.
They're in the scorpion family,
but they don't have venom!"
and "Yes, there *are* crocs also
at the dormant volcano
in the middle of the lake
that's as large as Long Island
that we'll be climbing down into tomorrow,"
and "Yes, I did see baboons
attack a family with small children
and try to steal the baby,"
and "Yes, there are lions,

but we don't see them,"
and "Yes, we are camping
in the desert for two nights,"
and "Yes, one of the other girls
did get malaria, *but she survived.*"
And "Yes, terrorists
did lob a grenade
into a nightclub in Nairobi,
killing sixteen people,"
and "Yes, that's where we'll
be flying out of,"
and "Yes, Dad, I'm safe, Dad,
really, really safe."
And finally, "I hope I've been
able to allay some of your fears, Dad.

"But, *I'm* coming home, Dad.
I'll be all right.

"But I'm a cup full of sorrow, Dad,
because the people who live here,
will never leave here,
and will continue to eat
the sand for breakfast
and the wind for dinner."

The Wedge & Winds of War

The Flatiron Building
divides and conquers
wind people taxis buses
Broadway and 5th -
as this gargantuan cheese
wedges its way north.

They say that in the '40s
cops rousted men
who lingered too long
on one side or the other
of the building, where the wind
decided which way
to inflate a skirt
or to get a quick
flash of heaven
before some copper,
wielding a billy club
clouted one or two of them.

And sometimes the skirts
billowed like parachutes,
legs drifting down through
the scratching trees, onto the farms,

the waiting ack ack guns
in France, Poland and Germany
waiting for them.

Who then could not forgive them
their minor indiscretions
of what might one day be
their final earthly pleasures.

Any problems, let me know.

A Story of Fish & Blood

The old men, she said.
They can never get it up.
The desire is there,
but not the blood.
Sure, it'll be there for a couple of seconds,
but it fades quickly.
I watch them dress,
grief seeping into their faces,
the stammering:
B-but, I took a Viagra!
The embarrassment as they
scramble for their pants,
stowing their small failures.

But there's always another fellow behind,
two lines of old men stretching beyond sight,
one approaching, another receding,
like waves coming -- almost --
and going, a sea of sadness,
fish out of water--
water out of fish.

But they all leave scaled,
each of them deboned.

Drinking With Disney Characters

I am tearing down
Robert Frost's fences.
They are rotten with mold,
crumbling to the touch.
I'm taking the road
that's available,
because the others
are cholesterol clogged.

I don't need to kneel
at anyone's feet
to accept brimming spoons
of vitriol.

I've got a pint of it
in my back pocket
that I'm sharing with
the younger dwarves,
and we are chugging
deeply.

The Tower

…winks its message to us
through the dark of our
bedroom windows.
Its Morse code,
a message I can't
decipher other than
"Don't…"

How cryptic the planes
that float past,
and of course,
the occasional wandering
Cessna single engine
that hums its way
too low and flips
everyone from the safety
of their warm complacent beds.

Family Vacations

It's not how many hours you can stay awake,
after not sleeping for 24 of them,
what with the time changes
and the layovers, but how many
minutes you can stay awake at each curve
going 80 mph in the rental, hoping to keep at least
one of the blinds up with the wife and the
three daughters, single digits, *sound* asleep and
the road and the dark night and the longing,
the black & blue yearning for a bed,
a respite, a tongue in your mouth that
could wag out a song to keep you alert,
while the others move restively,
then come to rest again.

How little they know, in the cocoons of
their sleep, how close they are to the railings,
to the cliffs, to the rental car somersaulting
down the side of the mountain,
then the firemen lowering themselves on lifelines
to the burning wreckage, the screams subsided now.

And this…this is what keeps you awake,
alert, and all of them alive.

And they will never know
this hour, this minute, this second,
as later they sail off to ballet and tap,
twirling and gymnastics,
on into their lives and marriages,
to their own families,
as you drive, each year,
closer and closer to the edge
of that harrowing cliff.

Pramila Venkateswaran

Suffolk County Poet Laureate 2013-2015

I am an idealist who believes that art is radical in its ability to heal and possibly transform the artist as well as the reader. As an artist I feel I have the responsibility to describe social and political events around me. Art is ultimately political: I write about women's lives, their voices raised in protest, their power and their victimization. My poetry ranges wide, giving voice to hunger strikers, to the suicide of farmers as a result of the unfair global free trade practices, to the beauty of watching my daughters grow up. I use humor, myth, dialogue to get to the heart of a poem, play with words to make them sing.

I am lucky to be part of a community of poets on Long Island. Giving readings and workshops and highlighting poetry on the calendar of activities as well as calling attention to it in the media is a political act. It counters the violence that surrounds us and infiltrates our lives. For our community of writers, poetry matters; it is a panacea, both internal and external. Being poet laureate allowed me an insight into the value of poetry as I brought it to many venues, including places where poetry is unusual—farms, beauty salons, schools, veterans' homes, wineries, and churches.

Walls

I don't want to write about walls.
The word "wall" stops me in my tracks.
My imagination halts.
I feel suffocated.
I am tense.
A caged animal prowling around
in my enclosure.
Crazed.
Rage spurring me
to dash against the bars
and spill my brains.

I dream of open fields,
not even a shepherd's frail fence
to tamper the even green.

That our eyes can travel miles
discern pale objects in the distance,
chimneys, trees,
rooftops, clouds,
a storm,
a swarm of starlings
is astounding.

We love to stare and stare
to pick out the details.

Annie Dillard says it is indeed our poverty
if we cannot observe the small details that make our
world beautiful.

Walls are our poverty.
They gouge out the ground of our seeing.
Zen paintings etch the barest detail
inviting us to fill in large swaths of space
with our eyes.

We fill color and story
until the picture transcends its frame.
When we turn away,
the simple lines go back
to their places.

They hold the key to a world each one can make.

*

Walls refuse subtlety.
Walls are blatant.
They are inscrutable.
They are refracting mirrors,
so you glance away.
You find a detour:
How to get away and around
the obstacle.

Walls spur us to quest
for open spaces, see

the globe as a mass of heat,
air, light, and dark with no gates.

Like modern open-plan houses
where toilet stalls are seamless
with bedrooms and kitchen counters,
the outdoors traveling in, the indoors out,
a mysterious mesh.
A metissage.

*

The crow that dropped stones in the jar
so the water would rise up to quench his thirst.

The jackal who always found a way to capture his goal,
Or was it the fox?

The wise beast,
the Zen master,

the inscrutable riddle,
the mysterious, but, oh, so plain, answer.

We can learn from these.

Chipped Crockery

Praise chipped crockery left behind by grandmothers
and mothers in daughters' kitchens. Praise the cracks

meandering between blue rivers and mountains
etched on cups and saucers, teapots sporting dents

made at an anxious or impatient moment;
praise the declivity in the rim of a cup you place

at your lip, conjure up an ancestor lifting warm decoction
to her chapped lips separating like an anemone.

Praise the shattering, like sunrise on white Corelle
to remind you of that day, that moment, that story.

Who wants flawless china? Our speckled skin carries layers
of tales yet untold, calluses adding to the store of experience,

so praise the bruised, the dented, the stubborn stains.
Praise them, praise them.

Flight

A tiny packet of feathers
and twig-like bones
helps a bird sail
above the tallest pine.

My mind flies miles
when I examine
a philosophical
construction:

The walls of my
brain dissolve.
But language
        is a wall
        that limits my flight.

Lisp

My daughter could not say *stamp* and *post*;
instead she lisped *tamp* and *poth*,
could not pronounce *juice* and *shirt*
for she reduced *j's* and *sh's* to *th*,

so relatives' names, rechristened,
live on memory's nub;
a slight brush of its surface
and those childhood babblings fill
our vast word-built fen.

Black and White Pictures of Death Camps

Rows of tall pines have seen executioners
throw earth on twitching bodies. The trees
look stricken. They have heard shots ring out,
blue hour to bitter night.

It is easy to forget what joy feels like in the austerity
of the camps. Monastic austerity holds a glow.
But this starkness is hell only humans can make.

Why cry over dried flowers? makes no sense here.
The trees holding their breath, the grassy knoll
bearing the remains remember.

Mother Teresa's Sari

Perhaps her white sari with its blue border
makes you think of snow against sky,

but in Calcutta becomes smudged
with curry, medicine, and sweat.

Limitless the folds of her pleats, allowing
her to build an empire of service,

the edge of fabric hugging her shoulders,
tucked into her waist—no keys jingling there,

for this bride of Christ wears the soiled
V of her adopted country.

Sweatshop

On Sundays when dad cooked,
our kitchen became an assembly line.
Mother was banished to her room,
to be surprised later by his "delicious" cooking.
We were indentured servants at his
beck and call, chopping, grating, mixing,
washing, rolling our eyes and making faces
behind his stern back as he stood at the stove
commanding the stew to bubble and spurt,
holding his ladle like a scepter. "Jafaar,"
my brother whispered, as we slaved away,
obeying orders: "wash the coriander," "chop
the onion," "you've sliced the cukes too fat,
make them thinner," "where's the oil,"
"is this cumin or caraway seed," "why is
the asafetida lumpy," "why doesn't your mother
know how to keep the kitchen organized."
Where was the good fairy when we needed her?
When he ladled stew onto our plates,
we awarded him the silent medal for ineptitude

Robert Savino

Suffolk County Poet Laureate 2015-2017

A poet who prefers isolation, I have become a student of the Masters . . . learned from the dead poets, taught and encouraged by Long Island mentors. Poetry has become my work, everyday, anywhere, lured by life's landscape connections with the imagination.

Whitman was born here. O'Hara is buried here . . . and they have been succeeded by our mentors, who have established themselves and developed a contagious culture of Suffolk County poets, defined by their descriptive, imaginative creations; proud to share across boundary lines.

As Suffolk County Poet Laureate for 2015-2017, somewhere in the middle of it all, I believe the role to be not the one with the most books or the best poems, but an ambassador of our art. This has put me on the road to promote poetry and explore new opportunities . . . *miles to go before I sleep.*

Trail of Seeds

On the first day of my life
it was 54 degrees and drizzling.
I took my first breath then transferred
to the basinet showcase room

where you checked in with your mitt,
surveyed the birthplace conditions,
checked out with White Owl cigars
and headed for the ballpark.

It wasn't long before I learned
that after a certain age the pacifier
no longer takes off the edge,
and made mistakes . . .

though mistaken to think
all I was, was wrong.
There was Watergate & Deflategate,
 but from them came discovery . . .

as I discovered morals from your teachings.
I recognize that now, perched on a stump
beneath shadows of trees,
amidst the cold emptiness of winter.

I long for the warmth that surrounded
the tell-tale kitchen table.

I need to replace the stale bread
with a fresh, soft-crusted loaf

and seed the soil where you rest,
await the blossom of forget-me-nots.

Occupational Therapy

A businessman wakes to an alarm,
lathers to shave in the shower,
cleanse the grime of yesterday's toil.
He dresses in the suit his wife laid out,

Dashes past the kitchen table, fully set
and heads out to catch the rail,
briefcase layered with folders of anxiety,
fielding calls, texting responses.

The poet wakes sometime after sleep,
which could be anytime,
pours a mug of coffee
which might or might not be fresh,

Reads a bit, scribbles a few lines,
fills a backpack with unfinished pages,
then, silently sits beside the businessman . . .
his words speak volumes.

Breakfast With Sophia

She wakes on a bed in the living room,
in the dark. She crawls to the foot
and peeks over the edge to see
if I'd been to sleep at all,

then, unhinges into a series of karate moves
and says, "Grandpa, I'm gonna beat you up!"
I engage for a short while, then quickly take
to the breakfast table, a clandestine coward.

After one period of fruit loop table hockey,
she eats. I tangle with nocturnal words, aloud.
She lifts her spoon, holding it like nunchucks
and says, "Grandpaaaaw, you a knucklehead,"

then follows me everywhere, with her mother's eyes,
a pastime of summer fun, all over again.
When she leaves, flowers in the garden droop.
Crabgrass and dandelions peek out over the sod.

Imagine her return as a teen or young adult,
reading this poem to me or saying,
"C'mon Gramps, I can't dance to this!"

Composite Color

The night sky is black, perforated by bb holes
of light, sometimes under a blanket of doubt.
Perhaps it will change to African American night;
and Indian Summer to Native American autumn.

Why not . . . ask Crayola!
prussian blue changed to midnight blue
flesh is now peach
indian red, chestnut

and while green-blue, orange-red and lemon-yellow
were retired and enshrined in the Hall of Fame,
pink flamingo, banana mania and fuzzy
wuzzy brown were added to the list.

Segregation has become a tempered memory.
A double scoop of chocolate and vanilla,
once packed like fists of Sugar Ray
and Jake, now melts in handshakes.

Sammy and Frank; Martin and Bobby -
forging connections, a slow crawl
of tap dance steps to gigantean proportions,
a mixing bowl with no sense of separation.

Crayola brands, ice-cream stands,
playful minds, shaded hues of human

It's Not Always Black and White

He may have been born to a Yiddish speaking
family, though soon to become Rico Bandello,
Little Caesar, the tough guy, followed by
Bogart and Cagney, cultural icons of urban America.

High School dropouts became streetwise,
became earners in an era of post-war economic
turmoil, when I was to become a mere bloom,
part of a reproductive boom, and opt to inhale
the smoke of this socially defined New World,
until changes made me a marketable young monger,
a modest commodity of Machiavellian leadership.

Now, in the sunshine of fall years, I digress,
while FOR RENT signs splatter plate glass faces
of independent shop owner's dreams.
Airlines impose the pricing of amenities.
More commuters leave an empty rail car seat
to walk a beat of classified closed door mornings.

I've modified my once marketable red power tie
into a headband that holds back the sweat
of market schizophrenia, ever-raising taxes, etc.
The difficulty of getting past the straight edges
of this puzzle, race against the pace of my heart.

I retreat to the inner shell of my modest home,
mellow, to view a black and white movie.

Make No Revision

Once a year it's a requirement
of Catholicism to confess sins,
but I didn't know priests
can see you now as clear as
if it was the meat aisle
in Pathmark on Friday.
He never asked how long it had been.
It was written across my face;
but he asked how I've sinned.

Father, I've disobeyed Spell Check
twice-a-day; dangled participles regularly;
coveted O'Hara's lines once;
pirated Pound's words four times;
and stole the only copy of On the Road
from the local library in my junior year.
I'm envious of Rexroth and Rimbaud
and lust for lines that intoxicate
the atmosphere in the White Horse Tavern.

As an act of forgiveness, my son, gather
your thoughts . . . write one villanelle,
three haiku and one sestina.
You will not erase or strike out,
risk losing the moment of creation,
like this moment of confession.

Nassau County Poets Laureate

Maxwell Corydon Wheat Jr.

Nassau County Poet Laureate, 2007-2009

Being acclaimed by Paumanok Poets as Poet Laureate of Nassau County 2007-09 was an unimaginable honor. I use it all the time to underline the fact that the eastern half of Long Island -- Nassau and Suffolk counties -- is a powerful, identifiable American area of poetry, citing George Wallace, first Poet Laureate of Suffolk County.

All Long Island, from Montauk and the North Fork into Brooklyn, can be put into a geographic poetry unit across the river from Manhattan where there is a wonderful flow of accessible poetry events. Publishers have appeared producing attractive volumes of poetry by many poets in Suffolk, Nassau and eastern Queens Counties—even reaching into, Long Island's western region, Brooklyn.

And Long Island poets have found ways to form links and connections. Think, for example, of how poetry has been introduced to Sagamore Hill, home of President Theodore Roosevelt, by Linda Opyr, the third Poet Laureate of Nassau County. Poetry can be heard there at Christmas and other times.

A future is implied. I foresee a big meeting of Long Island poets laureate putting theirs and others' output together for all America to know and be influenced by. I am thinking more than the county laureates but of the many villages and towns that have artists serving as poets laureate.

Think of them all coming together -- from Montauk and the North Fork 100 miles from out in the Atlantic!

This is inspiring to me. It is my hope that my words, and this collection of poems, can be a great spark for that kind of gathering.

Snow Buntings

Grandmother shouts,
throwing her scarf over her shoulder,
pushing her woolen cap back,
leaning an ear into the storm.

"Over there, by the barn."
And I hear thin crystals of notes
falling through the snow.

"There they are," she points.
Birds in a swirl like blizzard snow,
wings unfolding patches of white.
"Snow flowers," grandmother says.

Orb Weaver

For Professor Frank Reiser

Aramenus emerges under August stars.
Her thread, a silken lariat in the breeze,
catches on the lawn chair,
a bridge she battens down.
She spins gossamer spokes,
orbits support lines around the inner regions
and around the outer, viscid trap lines.
She waits in the center of her universe.

Acid Rain

I have come to try my luck,
snapping out the line in soft loops,
easing the fly back across the surface.
The lake is a room that is all glass.
The trout would be inhabitants of another world,
except I don't see any.

Nothing has leaped at my lure.
No bullfrog has delivered a might 'jug-o-rum.'
No green frog plucked a banjo.
No yellow-throat scolded in the alder.

I have not seen tracks on shore,
not of raccoon, not of fox, not of deer.

The Lamps of America Were Illuminated With Whale Oil

They moved down from Greenland
off the New England coast
Off Amagansett, the Hamptons, the Rockaways
Herds of Leviathans
half mile off shore

The young watcher on the dunes
a morning in November
could see their wedge-shaped blows
the breaching of dark-toned tonnage
huge gnarled heads
mouths that were caverns of baleen

'Whale Off! Whale Off!" the Long Islander
would shout
cupping his mouth
his calls carried to the village
on Atlantic winds
"Whale off! Whale off!"

The shove of whaleboats through surf
men straining at long oars
their boats leaping

plunging into troughs
Harpooners balancing their bows

These mammals were the Right Whales
They swam slowly
They floated in their own streams of blood

Veteran

Man about twenty- eight
Leaves St. Bartholomew's Sunday breakfast feeding
crosses East 51st
Machine-knit red nylon cap covers his ears
sticky-brown, graying hair flares out
catsup-stained U.S. Army coat drags on snow
He grips his plastic coffee container

Harbor Seals In Winter

I look for them in Sag Harbor
the Great South Bay, Shinnecock Inlet

At Montauk, the hood of my green down jacket
snugged over my head, I walk
down the Sound shore

" Those are logs, " the boy says
when I point to seals hauled out on glacial rocks
One "log" rears
A wide, round head turns
Eyes from the northern sea focus on me

"Seal!"

She raises a flipper
Urges her thick five-foot body down rock
Swims off

The way the animal looks back
I feel she is summoning me
But the whiskered gray being
submerges below a snow- covered ice plate

Fascinating: mammalian blood
courses under arctic waters

Lycopodium

They are the elves' Christmas trees
Grandfather would say
of Ground Pine and Cedar
Once in the sun I laid on snow
eye level to see colored lights and bulbs
the size of frozen dew drops

They are lycopodiums, he'd say
teaching me again to pronounce the name
because scientific words have the sounds of poetry

Lie-ko-po-dee-um

You've got it, he'd laugh
his hearty red face broadening behind his white beard
his abundant frame frolicking

When I return home for the holidays
I always walk back to our woods
think of Grandfather assuring a small boy
Yes, I'll see that the elves have a happy Christmas

I am glad lie-ko-po-dee-um is evergreen

Gayl Teller

Nassau County Poet Laureate 2009-2011

Writing poetry and working with so many talented, perceptive people has deepened my empathetic response to all people and made me more aware of the common human family with shared frailties, needs, and dreams that cut across all our idiosyncratic differences of race, religion, and culture. Focusing on forgiveness in the laureate experience, with workshops emphasizing reading and writing poems from various perspectives on forgiveness, has helped me to understand poetry as the essential religion.

Jasmine

If I had to name it as fragrance,
I'd say it's that full-body spray, in winter,
after a long and achy jog,
its unexpected reachings
reminding me of my mother's Miguet,
her White Shoulders in my hair,
her perfumed bath soap sudsing,
giving off visible breaths of peace,
from farther than memory's headwaters,
through her long fingers, and I am
strangely refreshed on this coldest morning,
in this inhaled stillness.

And it's that ambling's sudden aroma, in spring,
from way down tangly, vined lanes with Mike,
where our Charleston's sweet, lush loving
is slipping, as an ambrosial fragrance
knows how to slip, unscathed and delicious,
through all those little, hurting thorns, along the road.

Along my heart's wild passageways,
there's a purely insinuating, sourceless scent,
I call it jasmine because it keeps learning another
way, another way, to catch me wholly
by surprise, and it's been meandering here a long time,
this richly exquisite, forgiveness tracery.

Memorial Day

From the middle school to the town pool,
down Old Country Road and Manetto Hill,
they march or dance or get wheeled
to Music in Motion, Weapons of Mass Percussion
playing "The Marine Marching Song,"
in peaceful celebration of our warlike nature,
for we're social, love fellowship, community,
and the sight of many people moving in unison
beneath the billowing, mammoth flag,
suspended in Olympic meaning over our heads
from two fire truck extension ladders,
and we townspeople have come to cheer
and witness in our darkened glasses,
with sunchairs and munchies, cameras,
and sunscreened kids with sippy cups,
and flags sewn onto their shirts and shorts,
strollers with strapped-in tots waving flagsticks
with Mickey Mouse and Lady Liberty,
one boy butting and bashing his super hero
enemy figures to the ceremonial tempo,
the reins of war playing in his hands,
some proudly strutting new acquisitions,
as a bevy of haltered adolescent girls
with red, white, and blue painted cheeks,

and some of us sit schmoozing along the curb,
wiling with anecdotes and strangers
in the joyous press of the flesh, brought
together and freed from daily routines,
in the hoopla a parade can bring
on a sunny day, in the vigor of the beat
of the military bands and commercial enterprise,
intertwined behind the police cars' flashing lights,
and they march or dance or get wheeled
past the God Bless America United We Stand
sign across the Plainview Water District's
sagging, chain-link fence, and so we
rise and applaud them, as they barely
graze awareness, passing in their uniforms,
with their covered scars, their unyielding visions,
their unhealed plans, the young and elderly vets
in motorized wheelchairs and off-white limos,
VFW, Navy, Army, Marine, Air Force
survivors from WWII, Korea, Vietnam,
Iraq, Afghanistan, with what covert corpses,
as we graze on snacks, what eyes blackened
at the side of the road, with what lingering
fears of roadside bombs, what silent
concoctions of antidepressants, what
new disconnects of telewar fighting
with joysticks and throttles from padded,
suburban seats, with what pride preventing
requests for help for swan dives from bridges,

what hard-wired empathy within military cadence,
with what is marching with them, hidden in plain view,
as the Cub Scouts march with Little Leaguers,
the Girl Scouts, Daisy Troopers, alongside cannons,
a 105 howitzer, with drab green tanks and jeeps,
then the Plainview Volunteer Fire Dept.,
the Red Cross and Seniors Helping Seniors,
a Long Island Bulldog Rescue truck
with two parading rescued bulldogs,
and then the glittery commercial vans and floats,
like Caruso's Pizza, Trio Hardware and Paint,
MAX Fitness led by kids in karate suits,
and a wide, street-consuming banner—
CELEBRATE REMEMBER FIGHT BACK
and hidden, as we graze, who dropped what,
let the plastic fly with newspaper discards
winging with Syrian civilian body parts,
jihads, Al Qaeda, Iranian nuclear upstarts,
movie ads for "Men in Black," where
evil has claws and oversized heads,
to be swept up another Memorial Day,
which everyday really is, with visions
of one inclusive human country in our heads,
but today we're here to have a good time?

Three Weavers

Someone has threaded a wee basket
securely through the branches of a tree,
and it has made all the difference
to the bird whose nest has fallen,
to that generous hand who held his own
quivering happiness as the bird's beating breast,
and to me weaving my afternoon's way
into that resonating vicinity
of secret little gift.

Worn-Out Walking Shoes

Who would have thought when I saved them
with an unwitting toss to this garage corner,
I would come to savor them later,
with their stained tongues loosened

over maws opened wide by many ingested miles
I walked, some alone in abounding sun seeking vision,
sometimes the inventor of my own cold, curable night,
or even on the underside of joy's hush, the great rush,

or felt their scraping down sudden drops
I never saw coming. What sloughed-off skin—
dried sweat-tears salt lick—defiant hues,
what dirty-sweet crumbs-grit—fur-blossom-bug bits—shit

got ground into the honeycomb fibers, the sole-treads,
what untraceable flecks make such a rich journey mulch?
Ground in, our grandkids' sweet ice-cream drippings
mixed with the rising beach sand, while we rolled

our bocci balls and roared with the untamed wind,
with feather barbs from the Flamingo Gardens Rescue Center,
where Mike and I hand-fed ibis and spoonbills
in the haven for the broken-beaked, the broken-winged,

and I walked among them, picking up the feel of their beings,
and from the company of each friendship, a little ship
moving me deeper into the currents of humanity,
as I tapped my feet and shook to the peppery beat

of the Dutch folksinger in the outdoor concert
at Grand Place, on our vacation in Brussels, last summer,
and exchanged addresses with the jovial woman akin to me,
photographed her baby with the dark eyes like ripe cherries,

ground in, the harbored tears of the lost Korean woman
we walked with for miles, till we found her hostel,
talking all that warm dark while without the same language,
with tears soaked up from strangers weeping together,

strangers from all around the world, stunned and aching
over naked human cruelty, depicted at the Anne Frank House,
so many tears, such living testament to human compassion.
Who would have thought how everyone who's ever moved me,

from everywhere I've ever been, in these worn-out
walking shoes,
would come home with me, rubbing through the skin of my life.
Who would have thought they would become like a child,
moving around inside me, keeping me awake at night.

Moving Day

On Evergreen Avenue, in three little rooms
of a Bronx apartment, with high walls,
stippled with gold leaf in the living
room and roaches in the kitchen, where four fit
into one bedroom, and then where they moved
their adult sleep to the living room convertible,

it began with excitement. The Castro convertible
was rooted out from the rug, as dad shouldered the rooms'
furniture around to the rhythms of mom's moving
visions. He steered chairs by their wings to walls,
where they lit with new-angled sun for months of fit,
their cracked plastic covers breathing as if living,

as we sat in a novel place, facing the living
window world, watching an inverted pail convert
bugs and straw into feathery flyers that fit
their alchemy through slits in our fire escape to rooms
of sky and cloudwalls. Half-opened, the window was a wall
with voices from kitchens and showers and lots with
    children moving

spokes and sticks, ropes and balls. Our moving
needed no van, just dad, who quietly carried his living,
moving letters and passengers, and mom's wallpaper-
covered cornices, the fireplace that converted
a light bulb's heat to the spokes of a wheel, from room
to room, a harnessed suggestion of fire fitfully

flickering with replenished visage, sweet comfit
for the imagination on moving day. We moved
with mom's seasons, country colors and roominess
transmuting the plaster with our one painting of rustic living.
Each wall got sent to its camp and conversed
with a fresh air. My grandparents moved to stonewall

the rent they couldn't pay. My parents moved to stonewall
the rent they could pay, to stretch to outfit
their lives and their children's lives with meager, convertible
furnishings, like hand-me-downs, the urge to movement,
to free what inhabits cramped walls, a song of living.
like birds that could build in a washbucket's straw rooms.

Now I pencil the Evergreen walls, its moving
light flitting across the infitted figures of living
and loving, converted by sacred shabby furnishings of
     inherited rooms.

Linda Opyr

Nassau County Poet Laureate 2011-2013

Poetry is the closest thing we have to alchemy. It enables us to transmute the ores of ordinary experience into the treasures of time-transcending art. As a poet, I have found this to be both my greatest challenge and my greatest source of joy.

When I share my poems with others, it is with the hope that I will enable them to transcend my experiences so that they may enter their own worlds more deeply, more fully. Glimpses of my world are intended to bring others more completely to the windows of their own experiences.

While so much of writing involves a solitary immersion in oneself, the role of the poet is to enable others to see the fulfillment which results from transcending that solitary immersion. The sharing of poems through publishing, reading and teaching enables others to see what they may not have seen before: that place in poetry where the ephemeral becomes the eternal.

I am both humbled and honored to have served as a Nassau County Poet Laureate.

For me, this opportunity was a once in a lifetime chance to share my love of this alchemy with others who delight in both the power and promise of poetry.

Pavarotti Is Dead

this week. And so
is my cousin. Diane

and I went to the Village
in the late Sixties,

wore beads we'd strung,
and walked barefoot

in Washington Square
among the chess players,

baby carriages, balloons,
a three-cup con.

And old men who sat on benches
and sang in voices so fine,

I thought I'd never forget.

Turtles

Old soldier,
old rock of the sea,

today I remembered a day
I thought would never end.

I was young, in love
where there was no love.

Waiting
with nothing to wait for.

Old shell,
why this day

when I've forgotten
so much of the journey?

Why do I return,
old swimmer?

Old soldier,
old rock of the sea

Why Me

Because I am the one
who carries the medicine
the whistle made from antler shed
the days spent in the green rain
of the green wood.

Because I am the one
who dreams of the drum
the voices of night
before night has come.

The one who steps from road into mist
Returns on hooves of darkness
to glimpse your wide eyes
in the light that brings you to me,

Then takes you away.

The Gulls

The sun-bellied gulls
twist and turn, writing
across the winter sky.

In their alphabet
of wing and glide,
I see no clouds.

Just so little time
to watch what we will
when we can.

The Stranger

Even a stranger sees the changes in a house.

One morning, glistening in sun, a metal ramp
stretches from the wood of a front door
to the blacktop where a car is still.

On another afternoon, black plastic bags,
like mourners, are lined at the curb,
next to a walker or mattress.

Even the darkness staring from windows tells of
the meal not cooked
the plates in their cupboard
the living room empty.

And the stranger who passes
is usually no stranger at all.

Fogbound

Houses rise, swinging their windows
like lanterns, doors shut tight.

I pass in darkness as I have before, glimpse
in silhouette a stranger, there, then not.

Tonight I'd give anything to hear the geese
or find halfway up a shrouded tree,

a raccoon who turns the fire of his eyes
somewhere near what could be me.

Grey Clouds

Grey clouds, seven small birds, greyer still,
circling like hands on an unseen clock.

My eyes travel their river of wind until
I know they've gone where I cannot go.

That night where they rest.
That well where they drink.

That sky where this sky leads.

Mario Susko

Nassau County Poet Laureate 2013-2015

After more than 60 years of writing, I find it increasingly difficult to talk about my own writing. I do not want to "preach" what poetry writing is, or should be, for in both cases I impoverish my own creative possibilities, or what's left of them. Poetry is a process that challenges both our capability to think and express ourselves, as much as our readers'. That makes a poet walk a thin, sometimes a precarious, line between what reality is and what our mind perceives it to be and makes it be, at least temporarily.

Perhaps that's what drove me, having been honored by the Nassau poetry community, to try and "convince" the County that its abrogation of poetic freedom was devastating for younger and, especially, future poets whose expression should rely on the sense of one's unchecked ability to say something, the very thing we often talk about when we talk about reality of our times. Although I was not successful in my "mission,"

I still believe that I spoke for our community of writers to which I am eternally grateful. To be accepted by your peers as a meaningful voice because of your freedom of expression has shown me that the Nassau poetry community is healthy and free, and in that sense I believe I have accomplished my goal.

Life

Grandmother and I shared a small crammed room.
I slept on the sofa, she, in a high white bed.
She died when I was thirteen years old.
It was a cold gray January afternoon,
the kind that made your nostrils glue together
and the eyes burn from the coal smoke
belched by asthmatic chimneys in the street.

I came home from school and found my aunt
Sitting on a rickety chair in the hall.
She pressed my stiff hands against her cheeks,
whispering, You'll be alone tonight, my dear,
but I thought only of her soft velvet skin.

She took me into the room and to the bed
where my grandmother lay in her long blue dress,
with a small bouquet of satin violets on the pillow
and two wavering candles on the marble top table.
The curtains were drawn, the wall mirror covered.

It was grandma's shoes that kept me transfixed,
pointed black caps sticking up like crows' beaks,
and when my aunt went to close the cupboard door
which always squeaked open on its own

I spat silently three times to chase away bad luck.

The cupboard was a giant magic hat, things inside
never seen, like a gold rabbit foot she smuggled
through the German checkpoint, an endless source
of her night stories. After each she'd kiss me
and say softly, Adessodormi e fai un bel sogno.

My mother was to arrive by a late train, so I
had to sleep at my place. I stood guard, the major
in the third room, requisitioned for war veterans
by the commissariat, listening to patriotic airs.
I pretended to be asleep when mother tiptoed in.

I tried to remember every song my grandmother sang
to me in Italian, about her homeland, lost love,
and that morning I awoke in the frigid room, alone,
with a shameful erection. I propped myself up,
looking at her waxed face, and saw her wink at me.

Two days later I raided the cupboard, digging
out a pistol lighter, cancelled banknotes, letters,
sepia photos of sailing ships, a cracked telescope,
and old broken compass; I got so angry I ran down
to the shed in the yard, dragged out my treasure,
a wobbly corroding bike with no brakes, and rode it
around the oak tree until I was blinded by tears.

Checkpoint

at the checkpoint made of tree
trunks and barrels filled with sand,
a group of pale bus riders standing
in a meandering line depends
on one man whose belly will
soon have his blouse buttons burst.

am I a Jew, a Muslim, a Catholic,
which one does he wants to hate more
today: will my name on the soiled piece
of paper confuse him or make him
pull me out by my shirt sleeve
as if I were a disposable part

of the human race, deemed perhaps
to be worthy of living or dying,
as my uncle used to say, by the look
of my penis: am I saved or doomed
if he suddenly remembers, or I do,
that we went to the same high school:

as I try to keep my sternomastoids
from twitching. my mind from being forced
to accept that someone who has no power

over life is a bigger coward than someone
who does, he positions himself before me,
hissourish breath becoming my breath:

Do you know if Maria's still there:
his words burn on my face like amber:
there, meaning in the city: and I feel
cold sweat run down my spine: am I
done for if I say yes, or if I say no,
pretend I did or did not recognize him:

but he just grins and hands me back
my papers, moving to a young woman
next to me and motioning with his hand
for her to step out, still glancing at me,
while I rock back and forth, staring
past him, past my life, at the jagged line
of skeleton trees on the mountain ridge
where the dying daylight still lingers.

Plots of Life, Plots of Death

my dead mother undoubtedly did not
have money to rent her grave for good,
and I have never been there to know
which grave was hers, which bones
now in a common grave to which she
has been exiled could be hers, and
even if I did, would I be able to verify
that, or simply take someone's word for
it, Here's your mother's rib and the rest,
not much is left, things get misplaced or
even lost during moving, but you can
do with these whatever you wish.

throughout her life she was patiently
buying foot by foot of her cemetery
plot, monthly payments neatly recorded
in her book, and come each Christmas
she'd let me know, Most people die
at this time of year, isn't that strange,
but if I go I have my final resting place.

You have nothing to worry about
while I'm around, my assurance no
more than a naïve insurance that life

and death were part of an orderly
though not fully predictable plot.

she ended up dying at a place
of her exile where that little book
was of no value, and I live at a place
of my exile without a book or a plot.

and that's pretty much it, the whole story
about planning for one's future after
death or hoping death will pass by if one
does not have anything to plan for.

A Shortcut

I woke up one night to find
an angel sitting at the foot
of my bed and holding my coat.
I came to take you with me,
he said. You have suffered enough.
It's time you have some peace.

Was it necessary for you to come,
I asked. He smiled, or so I thought,
And said, Would you like someone else?
Snapping his invisible fingers, he
turned into a reddish burly man
I met in a bar once who claimed war
was a historical necessity to clear
the air. Truth, he exclaimed, is
at that point completely irrelevant.
He raised the glass, his little
and ring finger curiously hidden.

I can be your father, the angel
said and I heard the shoes click.
His torso swayed in the air, my coat,
over his shoulders now, resembling
the wings of a giant bat. The shoes

go click-a-click, the angel chanted,
and save the owner's life, your life,
my life, in the steamy Obersturm-a-
sturm-and-bon-a-bann-fuhrer's office.

There suddenly was humming behind me,
and, turning, I saw camouflaged trees
advance toward me, the ghosts
dancing to the beat of his song.

Let us go, the angel said. We have
a train to catch, so we'll take
a shortcut. I looked at the mine
field ahead and then at him again.
Don't worry, my friend, he whispered
and winked, or so it seemed to me.
Nothing ever killed a man twice.

I took a deep breath and followed,
my airy legs almost waltzing.

Conversion

I came upon a man in black who sat on a tank,
tending his sheep that grazed impassively
around the craters and among dead bodies.

I am looking for my son, I said squinting.
The bullets in his cartridge belt slung
over his shoulder shone in the sun like teeth.

He smiled, chewing a cigarette to the other
corner of his mouth, and motioned with his hand
to the field. Plenty to choose from, he said.

The sheep were moving away toward the shade
of a big oak tree, the bodies following
on all fours. I strained my ears to hear the bell

I knew. He slid down and stared at me.
Is that your stomach growling, he asked.
I am just trying to find my son, I whispered.

You want me to shoot one? He spat out the butt
and stomped it with his boot that was like my son's.
We are talking about some good meat, he grinned.

The shirt looked familiar, but I couldn't tell.
My sheep started to fan out and I suddenly heard
a dog yelp behind me. He whistled, the sound

thin and piercing, making the bodies stop.
I felt the sweat run down my buttocks and legs,
as if someone was punching holes in my ribs.

Have you seen my son, I uttered, not knowing
whether any sound left my mouth. You never had
a son, he yelled and cocked his submachine gun.

The boots were the same, and so was the shirt,
and the Mickey Mouse watch on his wrist was the same.
Tell you what, he said and laughed. I'll be your son.

Homeward Bound

I remember tomorrow, that was all
I said when I set out on the way home,
though, by the way, if there were a way by,
tomorrow must have already happened or I
would not have remembered it, which meant
even if I had arrived where I was supposed
to arrive, back home was there no more,
for I would've made it only to yesterday,
and wouldn't that have been the very day
when I said: I remember tomorrow –

still, I followed the rusty railroad tracks,
thinking they'd have to get me somewhere,
although they were overgrown with weed,
only here and there a meager looking flower
I hopped over or walked around, often losing
my step, until I came to a gate, a spider web
iron gate with a lock shaped like a heart
on a chain around someone's neck, but there
was neither a fence nor a wall at the right
or the left of it, except two track ruts going
on and fading into a breathing shimmering haze.

I stood there, to see whether another day,

the one before or the next, was on the other
side of the gate, but then a child appeared
as if he stepped through a curtain, jumping
unsteadily from one invisible sleeper onto
the other, from time to time flapping his arms
to maintain the balance, and he came to me,
his cheeks all puffed up, took a key
out of his mouth and unlocked the gate.
I could have gone around, I uttered, but he
smiled and said: Walls and fences are not absent
Because we do not see them, but you remembered
Tomorrow, so you can pass and go home with me.

he turned around and jumped onto the first patch
of scarred dirt, and I followed, the sleepers
getting farther apart, our leaps ever more daring,
and I waved my arms, and he flapped his, as if we
were going to leave the earth and fly up, still
two playful kids on their way home, not to be
caught out too late, overtaken by darkness.

Lorraine Conlin

Nassau County Poet Laureate 2015-2017

    I was chosen poet laureate because of what I have done for poetry. I support poets by attending their readings and inviting them to read at venues I host. I write blurbs for their books, arrange book launches and signings and promote their events. The poetry community has afforded me the opportunity to further grow poetry on Long Island. At workshops and open mics throughout the boroughs I meet new voices and invite them to join our groups and become part of the *Long Island scene*.

Listening to others read, attending workshops and critiquing at those workshops helps me to hone my craft and go beyond the borders of my creativity. I consider myself a poetry apostle and love spreading the word. Most of what I write is memories of my life and I enjoy sharing those memories and hope they are somehow relatable to readers and listeners. Our poetry community is special, it allows everyone to share and I am all about sharing.

As Good As Bread

(*Buono Come il Pane*)

As the train rolls past
the smell of bread fills the car
I see the old red sign
sigh at the thought the plant is closing
two-hundred livelihoods soon to be lost

Dad worked there thirty years
said his job was our *bread and butter*
brought home fresh-baked loaves
he removed from the ovens

He'd joke, "If it weren't for bread
you wouldn't be here."
He met Mom in a bakery
told stories of standing in bread lines
said, "A day without bread is long."

Dad loved bread
dipped the crusts and ends
cleaned his plate
never wasted

We broke bread, shared with others
thanked God for all we had
for our daily bread

Brass Ring

Sorting metals to recycle
I find an old tin coffee can
filled with remnants of
do-it-yourself projects --
door knobs, rusted hinges
fittings and one brass ring

My fingers circle the shiny thing
retrace merry-go-round memories
Rockaway *Playland*, Dad lifting me
to a carousel,
seating me
on pink mares or baby-blue stallions
securing leather straps
Telling me,
"Hold on tight!
Grab that ring!
You can do it, don't ever give up!"

Always cheering me on, clapping
each time I'd come around
his reassuring words,
"You almost had it this time"

I still hold tight
    Still reach further
        trying for that prize

Grapevine

I see Mom sitting alone
in her favorite spot
beneath the purple clusters
and I remember the sweetness
of the jelly and jam.

I could offer to make her some
but she would be bitter
reject it and me
say it is not like hers
and we would both hurt.

If her hands didn't shake
if she had more strength, less memory
maybe she would be happier.
I wouldn't have to
slow down when we walk
or go back with her to the place
that once was her smile.

If she could forget
some of the good parts maybe
life wouldn't be this tedious journey
taken time and again

when we visit
or when I'm alone and see her still.

Maybe if she
hadn't been everything yesterday
it would be different today
I could go there and leave
without thinking of her
sitting alone
staring at the grapes.

Looking For Nina

I used to say
I need this or that
always need
never want…

I had the need to justify,
thinking that want was selfish.
Friends said it was ok to want

Now when they ask me
"What do you want"
I tell them

I want a Sunday kind of love
lingering in bed
reading the New York Times
making love between sections
looking for answers
to 36 down and across
searching for Nina
hidden in Hirschfeld's
satirical drawings
agreeing what film to see
at the Waverly

afternoon walks
through Washington Square Park
ordering Shandy or a Black and Tan,
Stilton cheese and soda crackers
at the English Pub

train rides home
sharing…

That's what I want

Marlboro Man

At high school dances in the sixties
he held me close
left no room for the Holy Ghost,
a distance marker of Catholic chaperones

His rugged hands came to rest
on my shy-girl shoulders
his varsity-lettered chest
pressing my pubescent breasts

I'd inhale his *Canoe* cologne
and the ever-clinging seductive smoke
reined in by the weave of
his herringbone jacket and skinny silk tie

He was spicy hot and oh so cool
and I wanted to ride
with this rugged guy

We meet again in our sixties
the Holy Ghost, down-sized
by the Church to a Holy Spirit
and we, chaperones of
commandments and contracts

still holding close
dance apart
holding on

Hands

All you have to do is touch my hand to show to show me you understand and something happens to me that's some kind of wonderful
~ *The Drifters*

I see them still
holding me tight
locking me in a soft embrace
gently rocking cradle and carriage
soothing senses
wiping away fear and tears
brushing tangles of hair
combing curls around a forefinger
always stroking reassurance

I faintly hear hands
applauding my first steps
patting my back
lulling, like the language of poets
those welcoming waving
hands of hello
lingo laden fingers and wrists
letting go, saying goodbye

I've savored
the healing of tender hands
sentinels of safety, security
their sweet scent
nourishing finger-licks
dipped in confections of caring

Warmed by gloved thoughts
embedded in folds of life gone by
cuddled by past tense love
hugged with affection of old
I want, need and long for hands
to get lost again
in that some kind of wonderful.

Rockaway Of My Heart

June 24th
Feast- day of St. John the Baptist
first day of the season I'm allowed
to go into the water
at Rockaway Beach
I wade in
stop knee-deep
look both ways as if crossing a street
turn to see if Mom is watching
don't go too deep, I think I hear her say
turn around, see her handing Dad a sandwich
he's the one who catches my eye,
rejects her offering
runs to my side
leads me into deeper water
stands behind me
teaches me to face oncoming waves
bend, anticipate
wait for the right time to rise
keep my head above water
respect what I fear

I tire
waves break – crash – roll

upset my balance
face full of splash
I choke – cough – cry
he lifts me
higher each time
... so high
I can see the cloudless horizon
calm seas, floating gulls
... so high
I feel the warmth of summer
love

Acknowledgements

Lorraine Conlin

GRAPEVINE (Northshore Woman's Newspaper, Poetryvlog.com); HANDS (Performance Poets Association Literary Review); ROCKAWAY OF MY HEART (Paumanok Interwoven); WINTER NIGHTS (Avocet); LOOKING FOR NINA (Bards Annual 2015); MARLBOROUGH MAN (placed in Mid Island Y Poetry Competition 2013)

Tammy Nuzzo-Morgan

"NEWS FOR TODAY" (Suffolk County Poetry Review); "BENEATH AN IRISH SKY" and "THIS IS NOT YOUR POEM"(Mobius, The Poetry Magazine); "T[HE] [B[ONE]]": (FRESHET, Fresh Meadow Poets); "MAYBE SOMEDAY I WILL GET IT RIGHT" (The Southampton Review, Chickenpinata);

Linda Opyr

A SMALL POCKET OF BIRDS, AUGUST, BEFORE I WAS AFRAID, FOGBOUND, PAVAROTTI IS DEAD, TURTLE, GREY CLOUDS (The Ragged Cedar, Writers Ink Press 2012)

Robert Savino

BREAKFAST WITH SOPHIA (Oberon 2008, first prize); MAKE NO REVISION (Oberon, 2012); COMPOSITE COLOR (North American Review, 2010);

Mario Susko

LIFE, A SHORTCUT, CONVERSION (Eternity On Hold, Turtle Point Press 2005); CHECKPOINT (Closing Time Harbor Mountain Press, 2008); HOMEWARD BOUND (Framing Memories, Harbor Mountain Press 2011)

Gayl Teller

"WORN OUT WALKING SHOES," "THREE WEAVERS," "MEMORIAL DAY" and "BUILDING A CHIMNEY (Hidden In Plainview, Word/Tech, Cherry Grove 2015); "JASMINE" (Inside the Embrace, WordTech/CherryGrove, 2010 and Toward Forgiveness, An Anthology of Poems, Writers Ink, 2011); "MOVING DAY" (One Small Kindness, Plain View Press, 2003)

George Wallace

A SIMPLE BLUES WITH A FEW INTANGIBLES, JONESING WITH MOSES ON THE HIGH TIDE LINE, LIKE A PEACH TREE BLOSSOMING IN WINTER RAIN and OFF ROAD FOUR WHEEL BUSTED UP COLLARBONE ROLL BAR MISS AMERICA (2016, A Simple Blues With A Few Intangibles, Foothills Publications, 2016)

Maxwell Corydon Wheat Jr.

VETERAN (Iraq and Other Killing Fields: Poetry for Peace, Sheron Enterprise 2004); SNOW BUNTINGS, ORB WEAVER, ACID RAIN (Trillium, 1985); THE LAMPS OF AMERICA WERE ILLUMINATED WITH WHALE OIL, HARBOR SEALS IN WINTER (God-Hawk, 1992); LYCOPODIUM (Following Their Stars: Poems of Christmas and Nature, Cow Meadow Promotions, 2000)

Afterword

The Poets Laureate have a very important job. Not only are they meant to spread the love of poetry throughout their given areas, but they are intended to be examples. They are the ones that all eyes are on--they are the ones that other poets look to, to learn from, to aspire to be like, and to lead the way.

We are lucky that on Long Island we have been blessed with many amazing examples in the form of our Laureates. They host readings, they give workshops, the publish anthologies and hold contests. They are always providing opportunities for those wishing to walk the path of the poet.

The idea behind this anthology was to make it a little easier for the average person and poet to sample their amazing work, and get to know a little bit more about the people who make our community so vibrant. I thank George Wallace for servings as editorial advisor on this project, and I thank all the Laureates for taking part in this book. May it be used as a tool to educate and inspire.

~ James P. Wagner (Ishwa)

Local Gems Poetry Press is a small Long Island based poetry press dedicated to spreading poetry through performance and the written word. Local Gems believes that poetry is the voice of the people, and as the sister organization of the Bards Initiative, believes that poetry can be used to make a difference.

Local Gems is the sister-organization of the Bards Initiative.

www.localgemspoetrypress.com

Made in the USA
Middletown, DE
22 October 2022

13272708R00086